C000184838

Ideas for Appliqué

The Appliqué Artist's Workbook

Ideas for Appliqué

The Appliqué Artist's Workbook

Eileen Campbell

SALLYMILNER PUBLISHING

First published in 2008 by

Sally Milner Publishing Pty Ltd

734 Woodville Road

Binda NSW 2583 AUSTRALIA

© Eileen Campbell 2008

Design: Anna Warren, Warren Ventures Pty Ltd

Editing: Anne Savage

Photography:Tim Connolly

Printed in China

National Library of Australia Cataloguing-in-Publication entry

Author:	Campbell, Eileen.
Title	Ideas for appliqué : the appliqué artists workbook /
	Eileen Campbell.
ISBN:	9781863513883 (pbk.)
Series:	Milner craft series
Subjects:	Appliqué--Patterns
Dewey Number:	746.445041

All rights reserved. No part of this publication may be reproduced, stored in a retrieval system, or transmitted in any form or by any means, electronic, mechanical, photocopying, recording or otherwise, without prior permission of the copyright owners and publishers.

Disclaimer

Information and instructions given in this book are presented in good faith, but no warranty is given nor results guaranteed, nor is freedom from any patent to be inferred. As we have no control over physical conditions surrounding application of information herein contained in this book, the author and publisher disclaim any liability for untoward results.

10 9 8 7 6 5 4 3 2 1

Dedication

In memory of my mother
Rosetta Frances McIntosh
(Marnie)
an artist and an inspiration

Acknowledgements

A big thank you to all my students over many years for their enthusiasm and willingness to try anything new. It was their idea that this book should be written. Teaching has been an absolute pleasure and I have learned much from my students as well.

Thank you also to:

★ Sally Milner Publishing for having faith in the idea of this book.

★ Ivanhoe Girls' Grammar School for allowing me to use a detail of their quilt.

★ Susan Murphy for help with checking the text.

★ Mariya Waters for many encouraging coffee chats and quilting discussions.

★ My sons Derek, Alan and Neil, and their families, who are always so supportive and appreciative of my work.

The biggest thank you of all to Ernie, my helper and travel companion to teaching venues far and wide, organiser of exhibitions, builder of my new studio, sounding board, ardent supporter and constructive critic. It has been an amazing quilting journey together thus far. I look forward to the next adventures.

Contents

Introduction

Applique work is thought by some to be an inferior kind of embroidery. That is not so. It is not a lower but another kind of needlework, in which more is made of stuffs than stitches. In it the craft of the needleworker is not carried to the limit; but, on the other hand, it makes great demands upon design. You cannot begin by just throwing about sprays of natural flowers. It calls peremptorily for treatment—by which test the decorative artist stands or falls. Effective it must be; coarse it may be; vulgar it should not be; trivial it can hardly be. Mere prettiness is outside its scope. It lends itself to dignity of design and nobility of treatment.

Lewis F. Day, *Art in Needlework*, 1908.

The term appliqué comes from the French word *appliquer*, meaning 'to put on' or 'lay on' or 'to apply'. One dictionary definition of appliqué is: 'ornamental work in which fabric is cut and attached, usually sewn, to the surface of another fabric to form pictures or patterns'.

Applique has been done using various materials for nearly two thousand years. Possibly it originated as a means of using up scraps of precious material or as a method to patch holes.

Since ancient times many different materials have been used in appliqué, including leather, felt, beads, bark cloth, fish scales and leaves. They have been sewn onto almost any material that could be stitched on. Skins and furs were also used by early cultures for appliqué and inlaid work.

An early example of appliqué is a ceremonial canopy dated 980 BC, held in the Boulak Museum in Cairo. It was a part of a funeral tent for the Egyptian queen Esi-mem-kev. Made from gazelle hides and dyed in several colours, it is decorated with appliquéd Egyptian symbols including serpents and blossom shapes.

Appliqué craft in Egypt has a long history, and is still practised today by tent-makers. Originally their appliqué decorated the interiors of nomadic Arabic tents. Today there is not a big demand for tents so the tent-makers' skills have turned more to decorative household items. The colours they use are brilliant and the designs can have Islamic, Pharaonic, birds and folkloric themes.

For centuries, crewel embroidery was used to decorate linens and bed curtains in Europe, but starting in the fifteenth century appliqué began to replace the embroideries. From the mid-1600s printed chintz fabric imported from India, with designs mainly of flowers and birds, became available—but it was very expensive. *Broderie perse*, a French term meaning 'Persian embroidery', became the method employed to make the best use of this precious fabric. Individual flower motifs were cut and appliquéd to a plain white or unbleached muslin background, often with decorative stitches. The background could then be heavily quilted with elaborate designs.

In the 1800s appliqué quilting flourished in many places and some interesting forms emerged, many of them still produced today. The Kuna Indian women from the San Blas islands off the Caribbean coast of Panama wear beautiful blouses that are decorated front and back with reverse appliqué designs, called *molas*. Three or more layers of different coloured cloth are cut in patterns so that the layers of cloth underneath are exposed.

The Hmong tribespeople, originally from the mountainous regions of China, Burma and Laos, work in a similar way in reverse appliqué embellished with embroidery. It is called *pa ndau* (sometimes written *paj ntaub*) or 'flower cloth'. It is used for clothing, bed coverings, hats and also for beautiful story quilts.

By about 1870 the traditional Hawaiian quilt emerged. These large appliqué quilts are generally worked with a symmetrical design that radiates out from the centre. The pattern looks as if it has been cut from a folded piece of paper. Design motifs are usually based on the natural world—plants, flowers or scenery. Two contrasting colours are used, one for the background, one for the appliqué.

During 1846–52 the ladies of Baltimore in Maryland, in the United States were stitching quilts that were quite different to those in any other region. They became known as 'Baltimore quilts' and the style is still known by that name. These quilts were made with appliquéd blocks. Often many people contributed to a quilt and signed their names to their blocks—these became the famous 'Album' or 'Friendship' quilts. The appliqués were very detailed and beautifully stitched. The subject matter could be cut paper designs, maybe from *scherenschnitte* ('scissor-cutting'), as cut paper designs were very popular in that era, or chintz designs (based on broderie perse). Some were simple floral designs, either symmetrical or asymmetrical with one or two flower shapes. Others were complex, with flowers, birds, butterflies or fruit in baskets and cornucopias; still others were representational designs such as flags, buildings, ships or anything appropriate to a theme.

All these appliqués were stitched by hand. Today hand-sewn appliqué is still very popular but the invention of the sewing machine has brought with it more elaborate embroidery and machine appliqué techniques. Add to that the seemingly endless introduction of products in paints, fibres, foils, threads and such to the market today, and the possible combinations present a very exciting prospect.

Traditional geometric designs and patterns for quilts along with beautifully appliquéd Baltimore quilts are still very much a part of the quilting world today, as can be seen in almost every exhibition. Many quilts that are entirely appliquéd and tell a story or depict a scene are now also to be found, as the appliqué technique has become more popular and accepted over the years.

Although this workbook is about machine appliqué, much of can also be applied to hand appliqué. The first sections cover one basic process of machine appliqué followed by ideas and techniques that I have used in my own quilts.

There is always something new to learn or try and over many years of teaching my students have inspired and taught me much as well. Dip into the pages and see what inspires or works for you. Above all be prepared to try new ideas or products and enjoy your own creations.

Have fun with appliqué!

Techniques: The Appliqué Method

Using Vliesofix (or other double-sided fusible webbings)

There are many brands and types of fusible webbings that can be used for appliqué, ranging through light and medium weight to heavy weight—Heat'n Bond Lite, Vliesofix/Wonder Under, Steam-A-Seam, Steam-A-Seam 2, Fus-O-Bond and Appli-Kay Wonder, to name some of the products. A couple of these have sticky backs after the appliqué shapes have been cut out and the backing paper removed. This means that you can 'audition' them in position on your background fabric before heat-fixing them with the iron. Read the instructions on the packet to choose the one most suitable for your project.

I often work with fine cottons and silks, sometimes fine synthetics, and find Vliesofix/Wonder Under the most suitable product for fine fabrics. This product has very fine glue bubbles on the back, which means that you never see any glue spots showing through on the right side of fine fabrics. For ease and consistency I will refer to Vliesofix throughout the text, but one of the other products may be substituted, particularly if you need a heavyweight fusible.

Tracing the design

Vliesofix is double-sided fusible webbing with tracing paper on one side. It makes appliqué very simple, provided you remember one thing—your design must be drawn in reverse on the Vliesofix.

To reverse the image, hold or tape the design *face down* onto a light box or a window with the light shining through it, and place the Vliesofix over it, tracing paper up. You will then be able to easily trace the design. Sometimes you will need designs facing both ways—for example, leaves that are asymmetrical or birds or animals that will face opposite ways in a design. In that case, place the design *face up* on the light box or window.

Each part of a motif must be drawn separately. Where one piece adjoins another, allow a margin of up to 5 mm (¼ in) on the piece that will underlap the front piece. This is necessary so that all the pieces can be firmly stitched to the background fabric without any gaps or raw edges showing. It is easiest to draw a dotted line for the underlap on your original design, and include it on your tracing.

Step 1: Design with the underlaps marked.

Step 2: Draw pieces separately in reverse.

Trace the pieces including the underlays onto the Vliesofix paper. If you have many pieces to be cut from the one fabric—for example, a group of flowers—you can trace them in a block and handle them as one at this stage.

There is no need to consider the grain-line of the fabric when positioning the traced design pieces. You can take advantage of the patterns in the fabric or just place the pieces for the least wasteful use of fabric.

Cut out the traced motif, leaving a small margin all around.

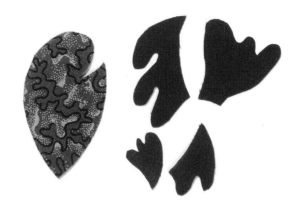

Step 4: Cut out.

Attaching the Vliesofix

Using a medium-heat dry iron, fuse the rough side of the Vliesofix to the back of the appliqué fabric. If you are working with synthetics or other delicate fabrics, remember to protect them from the direct heat of the iron with an appliqué mat or silicone paper. Cut out the traced shapes exactly from the fabric.

Step 5: Assemble the pieces on the background and fuse in place.

Step 3: Iron on to the reverse side of the fabric.

Positioning the appliqués

Decide where you will place the shapes on the background fabric. At this stage, you may find that you need more or less pieces, especially if there are flowers or leaves in the design. Be prepared to adjust your design according to the overall effect.

Peel the backing paper from the Vliesofix on each of the appliqué pieces. Making sure that all the underlaps are in place and each piece is situated correctly, use a medium-heat dry iron and press the pieces into position on the background.

A motif constructed with many pieces can be put together first on an appliqué or pressing mat. Peel the backing paper from each piece and assemble the motif matching the pieces to the original pattern. Fuse as you go. When finished, allow the motif to cool for a few seconds, then peel it off the appliqué mat and press the complete motif into place on the background. This is much easier than attaching it to the background piece by piece.

Step 6: Stitch to background and glue on the eye.

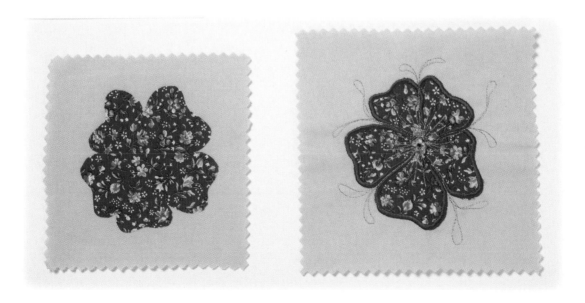

A single motif can be transformed with stitching and beads.

Stabilisers

Iron-on tearaways

Appliqué involving machine-stitching requires the use of an iron-on stabiliser. Before beginning any machine stitching your work should be backed with an iron-on stabiliser that can be torn away once you have finished stitching. If the fabric is not stabilised the stitching will pull it out of shape and it will never sit flat.

There are a number of different stabilisers on the market, but note that many of them are *not* the iron-on variety and are intended for use in a hoop with automatic embroidery machines. This type will not hold appliqué work firmly enough.

One of the most useful iron-on stabilisers is Vilene's Stitch'n'Tear Fusible (also known as Tear-away Bu8030). It looks and feels like waxed lunch wrap. The smooth side is ironed to the back of your background fabric.

Some products adhere more firmly than others. Be careful not to 'burn' the stabiliser onto the fabric as it is very difficult to remove. Use just sufficient heat to fuse it to the fabric, and tear it away immediately after stitching.

Stabiliser should extend at least 2.5 cm (1 in) beyond all the appliqué pieces. This will give a firm base on which to appliqué and free-machine stitch.

If you have a large design, it is often easier to work in sections and stabilise each part of the design as you go. With large motifs it can also be helpful to tack around the edges of the stabiliser, as larger pieces have an annoying tendency to either peel off or get caught under the presser foot as you

stitch. Satin stitch the appliqué pieces into position and complete any free-machine embroidery.

Take great care when you tear the stabiliser away from the back of any embroidered areas. Hold the embroidery stitching with one finger while you carefully tear around it.

Iron-on Vilene

Iron-on Vilene is used for three-dimensional appliqués or in any place where you want the extra support to remain permanently. It is left in place, not torn away when the work is completed. Medium to heavy weight iron-on Vilene is the easiest to work with. However, the light weight one gives a lovely soft finish and you can use two or three layers to give more stiffness. Iron-on Vilene has a grain-line so if you do use two or more layers, iron the second layer with the grain-line at right angles to the first. For three layers, the third layer will be laid down in the same direction as the first one. This will keep your work flat.

Broderie perse appliqué

The broderie perse technique was used in many old quilts to take advantage of the designs that were printed on Indian chintz fabric. Instead of drawing your own designs you make use of a design that is printed on the fabric. You can cut out birds, flowers or other motifs and use them either by themselves or with other designs that you have drawn.

Fuse a piece of Vliesofix to the back of your chosen motif before you cut it out. Use a narrow satin stitch to attach the motif to the background. Remember to leave an underlap if part of the motif is to go behind another piece.

Back fabric with Vliesofix and cut out the cats.

Put them in a boat and stitch.

Making a sample

Sample with notes for *Reptiles on Centre Stage* border

It is always a good idea to make a sample or test piece for each new project. I find that something about A4 size is quite sufficient.

Put together pieces of the background fabric and the stabiliser (or stabilisers) that you are planning to use in the project. If you are using the absolute last piece of a special fabric or have not got enough to spare for a sample, you can use a substitute fabric of the same weight and type. Fuse some appliqué pieces to it as well. Using this as a base you can test machine settings, stitches, thread colours, and anything else that you have to make a decision about.

Write on the sample what the machine settings, stitches and threads are, and you have a record of what is right for the project. This will save you much unpicking on the real thing.

Sample with notes for *Pelican Twilight*

Border detail from *Reptiles on Centre Stage*

Stitching the Appliqué in Place

The sewing machine

Always make sure that your machine is totally free of lint around the bobbin case. Clean it thoroughly before using it and after every few bobbins, especially when sewing through layers of Vliesofix and backings. Keep the machine oiled according to the manufacturer's instructions.

Feet

★ Use an appliqué or clear plastic foot for satin-stitching. An open-toed embroidery foot is also excellent, as you can see your stitching clearly.

★ For attaching braid use a braiding foot; for wider braids an open-toed embroidery foot will help guide the braid through.

★ Use a darning foot for embroidery, outline quilting or free-motion quilting (Cornelli work or stippling).

★ A walking foot is invaluable for straight or gently curved quilting lines. A walking foot feeds the layers of fabric evenly through the machine, eliminating bubbles on either side of the quilt sandwich. Some machines have an even-feed foot built in instead of a walking foot. If your machine has this it should be engaged.

★ If your machine has a control for adjusting the pressure on the presser foot, then decrease the pressure a little for satin-stitching as this allows you more freedom of movement with your fabric.

Needles

★ For appliqué and machine embroidery it is best to use a Metalfil needle, size 75 or 80. This needle has a bigger eye and helps to stop the thread from breaking. It is especially good for metallic threads when appliquéing or quilting.

★ If you are satin-stitching or embroidering on silks or fine fabrics, a size 70 needle is good as it does not leave big holes. Match the needle and thread to the fabrics you are using.

★ When machine quilting with some of the thicker decorative threads, a size 90 needle may be required to stitch through the multiple layers.

★ The needle should be sharp and the correct size for the thread and fabric—a size 80 needle is good for most work. Change the needle after every six to eight hours of stitching, or more often if it becomes blunt.

Threads

★ For satin-stitching and machine embroidery the best results are achieved with machine embroidery rayon threads, especially for satin-stitching. These give a smooth even look with a lovely sheen that you cannot obtain using cotton threads, although these can also be used depending on the effect that you want. There are many brands to choose from.

★ A number 40 rayon thread is excellent and is the size most widely available. For more defined stitching, number 30 embroidery rayon can be used. For free-machine stitching that needs a heavier look, try a cotton thread such as Cotona 30, Sulky 30 weight cotton or a similar product.

★ A wide range of shiny metallic threads is available. The easiest ones to use have a smooth finish. These are excellent for highlights and special effects.

★ In the bobbin use Bobbinfil or a fine polyester or polycotton thread when appliquéing directly onto the background. The Bottom Line (a Superior Threads fine polyester) is designed for using in the bobbin or for fine appliqué and comes in a wide range of colours. Bobbinfil comes in black or white. If your tension is set correctly, you should be able to use white thread in the bobbin with light coloured top thread, and black with dark top thread, and not have it show on the top. Being very fine (number 70), the Bobbinfil helps to give a smooth even satin stitch with the rayon top threads. If you have trouble with the bobbin thread showing on the top of your work, one solution is to use the same colour thread in both the bobbin and through the needle.

★ For three-dimensional appliqués it is best to use the same thread through the needle and in the bobbin as the colour will then be even on all visible edges. When using rayon thread in the bobbin, wind the bobbin a little more slowly than usual so you do not stretch or break the thread.

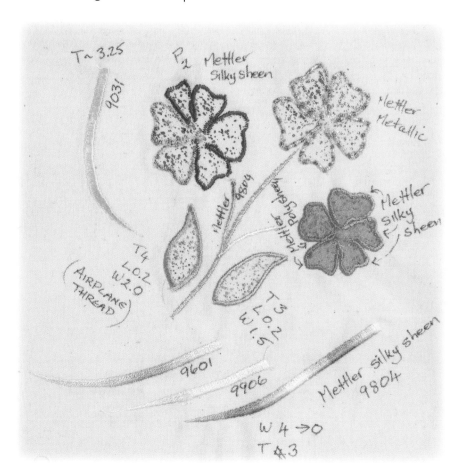

Test new threads and keep a record, including thread tension adjustments.

Satin Stitching

Because satin stitch plays such an important part in appliqué work, it is essential to get it right. This may involve you in considerable experimentation, and is where the value of sample pieces is fully realised.

The first step is to check your machine manual for the manufacturer's recommendations for satin-stitching, although you will often find that the top thread tension will have to be adjusted to produce a smooth even satin stitch without any bobbin thread showing.

To do this, loosen the top tension a little. For example, if the normal setting is 4, then reduce it to 3. If your machine has + or – on the tension dial, then move it toward the minus sign. You may find that you need to reduce the tension even more than this. Stitch a test piece, using stabilised fabric with contrasting threads in the top and the

bobbin. Take it out of the machine and look at the back. Your aim is to have the satin-stitching pull underneath slightly, so that the top thread can be seen on either side of the bobbin thread. There will probably be more top colour showing along one side than the other. If the top thread is not being pulled through enough, lower the bobbin tension a little more and try again. Keep this test piece and write your settings on it so that you have it as a reference.

On some machines, threading the bobbin thread through the special hole for buttonholes has the same effect as loosening the top tension. You may or may not have to adjust the top tension a little more.

What you are trying to achieve is zigzag stitches that are close enough together to appear as a solid line but not so close that the stitches bunch up and jam the machine. There should be enough

Concave curve. Stop and pivot on the appliqué.

Convex curve. Stop and pivot on the background fabric.

distance (length) between the stitches so that if you let go of the fabric the feed dogs will push the fabric through the machine without any problem. This will vary from one machine to another. Again, check the machine manual for the recommended setting but be prepared to adjust further to get the stitch you require.

The complex mixture of fabrics in a project can affect the machine settings required, so practise sewing on samples of the layers of fabrics and stabiliser used in a particular project. This will allow you to test tension, stitches and thread colour.

Satin stitch should rest mostly on the appliqué piece, coming over only slightly onto the background fabric. For most appliqués the satin stitch width is between 1.5 mm and 2 mm (up to $1/16$ in). With bigger motifs a larger stitch can be used. At less than 1 mm ($1/32$ in), the satin stitch becomes too narrow to hold the appliqué in place. For appliqué pieces that are very small it is better to use free-machining. .

Begin and end the stitching with a few fastening (straight) stitches on one spot. Lift the presser foot and move the work very slightly forward so that the first zigzags cover the starting point. To finish off, lift the presser foot and put the fastening stitches just behind the last couple of stitches, or stitch in one spot right beside the zigzags on the appliqué side. Alternatively, pull the top thread through and tie it off at the back. Do not stitch forward and back over the satin stitch as this will create a lump.

The aim is to sew at right angles to the edge of the appliqué piece you are stitching. Where you need to change the angle to go around a curve, stop with the needle in the outer side of the curve, lift the presser foot, turn the work slightly and do a few more stitches. Repeat this pivoting step as many times as you find it necessary to complete

stitching the curve smoothly. For a concave curve you will be stopping with the needle on the appliqué; for a convex curve the needle will be on the background fabric. With experience, you will find that you can control your stitching at a fair speed, turning the work as you go. This will eliminate some of the starting and stopping.

Using a 1.5–2 mm (up to $1/16$ in) stitch, it is not necessary to taper the points on leaves or narrow petals. Instead, continue to the top of the point. Leave the needle down and turn your work. Raise the needle and reposition the work so that your first stitching in the other direction covers the previous couple of stitches. This gives you blunt point and is very easy to do without affecting the good appearance of the motif.

It may not matter if stitching goes a little off line and moves too far onto the appliqué—for example, if it is a leaf or flower and the basic shape is not altered appreciably. In such a case, raise the excess fabric with your fingernail, and use a pair of very sharp scissors to trim it off.

If trimming the appliqué like this will spoil the shape, or if you have stitched too far onto the background and the appliqué is no longer held in place, you will have to take the stitching out and redo it. The easiest way to do this is to turn your work to the back and with a small pair of sharp scissors cut through the bobbin thread of the satin-stitching. Turn your work to the right side, pull the top thread above where you have cut and it should unravel like magic.

Free-machine stitching and embroidery

Free-machine stitching can be used for embellishing appliqués, stitching highlights and as an alternative method for attaching some appliqués. It is the same stitch as used for machine quilting. Providing you have a stabiliser on the back of your work, you should not need to use a hoop.

For free-machine stitching you will need a darning foot; you must also be able to lower the feed dogs or cover them with a plate. If this is not possible on your machine (or if fitting the plate does not leave enough room for quilting layers of fabric), one way round the problem is to cover the feed-dogs with masking tape. The machine needle will punch a hole through the masking tape as you stitch.

Set your machine for straight stitching. Turn the stitch width dial to 0 and the stitch length to 0. Tension should be normal, although you may have to lower it a little depending on your stitching. Bring the bobbin thread up to the top of your work and hold both threads as you take the first few stitches. After that you can stitch in any direction. It is best to run the machine fairly fast but this will come with practice.

If you have not used this technique before, I recommend that you practise on a sample piece before stitching on your project. Prepare some stabiliser-backed fabric, at least A4 in size. Practise going forwards, backwards, in circles, writing your name, 'drawing' flower shapes. Cover the whole of your sample piece.

Basic flower shapes.

Embellished with free-machining.

Fill in spaces or backgrounds with flowers and leaves 'drawn' randomly.

Stitch the veins on leaves.

Use free-machining to link flowers and leaves.

An entire appliquéd design can be free-machined.

1. Begin with flower shapes.

2. Attach them to the background with two rows of free-machining.

3. Embellishing the flowers and the entire stem and leaf designs forms the quilting.
They can be stitched in a heavier thread.

Free-machine stitching used to embellish simple flower shapes.

Using a darning foot

It is possible to take the normal foot off the machine and embroider without a foot at all but it is much easier and safer to use a darning foot. A darning foot usually has a spring that allows it to move up and down while you sew, although some machines have a different system to allow this. This gives support as the needle makes a stitch but allows you to move the fabric freely at the same time.

On most Husqvarna Viking machines, you must select the darning symbol, which will release the pressure of the machine foot on the fabric. Some Pfaff machines have a cradle position on the presser foot lever that lets you free-machine stitch without lowering the darning foot onto the fabric.

Check with your machine instruction manual or sewing machine dealer as different makes and models have different adjustments for embroidery.

Whichever machine and darning foot you have, it is essential that you lower the presser foot lever before you begin sewing otherwise you will end up with a terrible tangle of threads on the underside of your work.

The clam is made from suede and woollen fabrics Vliesofixed to a backing fabric and treated as a 3D piece. Free-machining gives definition.

Using a hoop

Using a stabiliser on the back of your work generally gives sufficient support when small amounts of free-machine stitching are to be used over an area, for example, when enhancing or attaching appliqués. However, if you have a large section of free-machining such as a bunch of gum blossoms, you may find that you need to use a hoop to keep your work flat even though there is stabiliser on the back of your work

Setting up a hoop for machine work is the opposite from setting it up for hand work. The fabric needs to be in the bottom of the hoop so that it will lie flat on the bed of the machine.

A plastic and metal spring hoop—either 13 cm (5 in) or 18 cm (7 in) diameter—is very easy to work with. It can be moved quickly and easily from one area to another and, with the fabric already stabilised, you do not have to be overly concerned about a very tight tension in the hoop as the embroidery is not very dense. If you are doing more elaborate embroidery, especially without a stabiliser, you will need to use a wooden hoop with a binding on the inside ring, which can be tightened by a screw at the side. A spring hoop will not hold the fabric tightly enough.

To set up work in a spring hoop, lay the plastic ring on a flat surface and place your fabric right side up over the top. Squeeze the two handles on the metal spring together and fit the spring inside the plastic ring so that the fabric is stretched evenly all round. Be aware that there will be one spot, just in front of the spring handles, where you will be unable to get the correct tension in the fabric, and position the area you are to embroider away from it.

Hand embroidery

If you use hand embroidery, either by itself or in conjunction with machine embroidery, three stitches you will find very useful are stem stitch, chain stitch and French knots.

Stem stitch can decorate flowers, create stems or add highlights of all sorts. *Chain stitch* is excellent for bird's legs. Outline the legs with a very narrow machine satin stitch, 1.5 mm (1/16 in), then fill in the shapes with fine rows of chain stitch, using a metallic thread. *French knots* can be used in flower centres and on wings. The possibilities are endless and of course many other stitches can be used.

Tumbling Fans detail. A variety of hand embroidery stitches have been used on this wool quilt.

Padded three-dimensional Blue Wren.
Made separately and attached after the quilting is finished and the braid is couched in place.

Three-Dimensional Appliqué

Three-dimensional (3D) appliqué can add great interest to a design. It is used for flowers, leaves or creatures which are held in place at one or more points, leaving some parts of the appliqué free-standing.

Follow the steps for the appliqué method up to the cutting out of the pieces, then proceed as follows: cut a piece of backing fabric large enough to hold all the 3D appliqué pieces plus 1 cm (3/8 in) all round. Choose an appropriate colour for the backing fabric if it is likely to show.

Depending on how firm you want the appliqués, cut either one or two pieces of iron-on Vilene the same size as the backing fabric and fuse it (or them) to the backing fabric. Consider using black or grey Vilene if your fabrics are dark in colour.

Peel the tracing paper from the Vliesofix on the appliqués and arrange them on top of the Vilene. Fuse them into place and satin-stitch or free-machine around them. If they are free-machined,

then stitch around the shapes twice. Some free-machine or hand embroidery can also be done at this stage. Keep in mind that you will use further machine embroidery to attach the pieces to the background.

Cut out the appliqués. It is easiest to use a small pair of sharp scissors and angle them underneath the work, taking care not to cut the appliqué threads. Leaving the tiniest possible margin of backing will help, and these tiny pieces will fall or pull away afterwards. If you do cut a thread—as nearly always happens—use Fray-Stop or clear craft glue on the end of a toothpick to prevent the stitches unravelling.

The cut edges of the Vilene can be coloured with a fabric marker pen that matches the appliqué colour. Double-ended textile markers are available in several brands (Fabrico is one) in a wide range of colours. If the project will not be washed, ordinary felt-tipped markers will do.

Stitched butterflies on the backing fabrics.

Cut out close to the stitching.

Pieces ready to be attached.

Free-form padded appliqué

The free-form padded appliqué technique can be used when you want even more definition or a greater 3D effect.

Prepare the pieces as for 3D appliqué, but using only one layer of iron-on Vilene. Cut a piece of iron-on Pellon the same size as the backing fabric and fuse this on top of the layer of iron-on Vilene. If iron-on Pellon is not available, cut a piece of Vliesofix and a piece of ordinary Pellon to the required size and fuse them together. Peel off the paper and you now have iron-on Pellon that you

can fuse to the iron-on Vilene. Use an appliqué mat or baking paper between the Pellon and the iron.

Peel the tracing paper from the appliqué pieces, arrange them on the Pellon and fuse them in place, again using an appliqué mat or baking paper. Satin-stitch around the edges and complete any embroidery needed at this stage. Cut out and finish the pieces in the same way as for 3D appliqué.

Medieval Inspirations detail. The brolga's body is a padded appliqué.

Attaching the pieces

Three-dimensional pieces are usually the last to be attached to a project, often after all the quilting has been completed. They can, however, be attached at any stage depending on the effect you are trying to achieve. For example, attaching a flower by its centre before quilting, lifting the petals and quilting underneath them will raise the flower more than attaching it after quilting. These contrast very well with flowers appliquéd directly on to the background.

Flowers and leaves can be attached to the background with the machine embroidery thread to be used for the stamens or leaf veins.

Attach flowers by their stamens.

Flying creatures are attached by free-machine stitching around their bodies. Depending on size, the wings can be left free or caught down at the tips, perhaps angling the wing against the background.

Monofilament nylon thread is very good for attaching creatures as it is not obvious. Bodies of creatures, birds or fish can be further padded as they are attached. Stitch halfway round the body, and insert a very small amount of Dacron filling. Push it into place using a satay stick or something similar and then finish the stitching.

Medieval inspirations detail.
Three-dimensional flowers

Use Monofilament thread to stitch around the padded fish bodies. Leave the tails and fins free.

Padded flowers and creatures on the background fabric

There are two methods of giving flowers a fuller, more sculptured look without making them three-dimensional.

Method 1

1   Draw the flower onto the tracing paper side of the fusible webbing.

2   Iron onto the flower fabric and cut it out.

3   Fuse this flower onto the non-glue side of fusible Pellon. Use an appliqué mat under the Pellon and on top of the fusible webbing. Cut out the flower.

4   Fuse the flower onto the background and satin-stitch it. It is helpful to use a satay stick to hold the edge of the flower in place as you stitch as it tends to spring out from under the presser foot.

Method 2

This method is easier for multiple flowers:

1   Fuse a square of flower fabric to one side of non-fusible Pellon.

2   Draw a flower or flowers onto the tracing paper side of the fusible webbing and cut out roughly, leaving a small margin all around.

3   Fuse the flower or flowers to the other side of the Pellon and cut out the flower/s.

4   Proceed as in step 4, method 1.

For birds or other creatures with many pattern parts, a third method is preferable.

Method 3

1   Construct them first on an appliqué mat or silicone baking paper.

2   Peel the completed motif off the mat or paper and fuse it to the non-fusible side of the Pellon.

3   Cut it out and proceed as for step 4, method 1.

A padded pelican.

1. Padded lily ready to appliqué.

2. The top lily has no padding so it looks pale. The two lower lilies are padded.

Heat-vanishing muslin

A very delicate effect can be achieved in insect wings and flower petals with the use of heat-vanishing muslin such as Thermogaze or Heat-Away. The muslin can be put into an embroidery hoop and embroidered by machine in the usual way. Subsequent ironing turns the muslin into a brown powder which can be brushed away.

1. Draw guide lines on the muslin.

2. Stitch the wings.

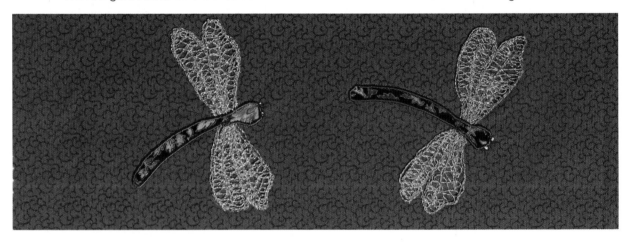

3. Heat away and add the bodies.

4. Stitch a feather star in two parts. Heat away and stitch the two parts together on the background.

5. A completed feather star.

Marnie's Seagulls Visit the Reef detail. Corals made with vanishing muslin.

When machine embroidering on muslin, use the same thread through the needle and in the bobbin, as both will be seen. You can draw on the muslin easily with a pencil if you need guidelines. Make sure that all embroidery lines are connected so that your piece will not fall apart when the supporting backing is removed; you can check on this by holding the hoop up to the light before ironing away the muslin.

Put the embroidered muslin between two pieces of silicone baking paper when you press it. This protects the threads from direct heat and catches all the powdery bits as they crumble away. The muslin turns brown as it is heated but keep checking to make sure you do not really burn it. A nail brush is handy for removing the last bits of powder.

To attach the embroidery, before or after quilting, use either the same coloured thread or clear monofilament thread and free-machine it in place. Leave some areas unattached for a three-dimensional effect.

Store heat-vanishing muslin in a dark place to prevent it from deteriorating.

Wash-away stabilisers

A butterfly stitched on Solvy.

Solvy is possibly the best-known wash-away stabiliser product for use in machine embroidery. Romeo is much thicker, and very strong. It can support any amount of stitching and you only ever need one layer. Guilette is a cold water-soluble medium weight film (half the weight of Romeo) but still has excellent strength. Heavy weight Water-Soluble Paper is a translucent paper which is stable and traceable. It dissolves easily without leaving any residue.

In general, a hoop is necessary when using a wash-away stabiliser, although Romeo is strong enough to be used without a hoop. To set up the machine, lower the feed dogs and attach the darning foot. Usually straight stitching is used, but good effects can also be achieved with a zigzag stitch. Stitch an outline of your motif first and then use various filling stitches between the outlines.

When stitching you must link all the lines of stitching together, otherwise the design will fall apart when the stabiliser is removed. Use the same coloured thread on the top and in the bobbin as both will be seen.

Before removing the stabiliser hold the design, still in the hoop, up to the light. This will allow you to check whether all the stitching is connected. If there are weak spots or loose threads, then add some more stitching.

Cut away excess stabiliser from around the design before dissolving the rest of it away.

Pin the embroidery out on a polystyrene tray before placing it in water so it will keep its shape. If this can't be done, you will need to block the design out before leaving it to dry. You can either hold the embroidery under cool to tepid running water or place it in a bowl of water.

Making use of scrap threads with Solvy
Collect the bits of thread that you would usually throw away. Arrange them between two pieces of Solvy and put them into a hoop. Tiny pieces of fabric or glitter flakes can also be added. Stitch over them randomly so that they are linked together. Take the threads out of the hoop and dissolve away the Solvy. Depending on the colours and arrangements, these threads can represent grass, branches or whatever you choose. Use further stitching to attach the piece to a background.

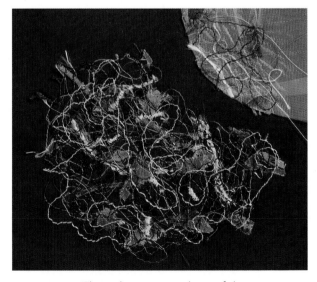

Thread scraps made useful.

Couching threads and braids

Thicker threads or braids that will not go through the machine, for example, those used for outlining panels or flower stems, can be couched down. Use a braiding foot, or guide wider braids under an open-toed embroidery foot using a satay stick or something similar—instead of your fingers—to hold them in place as you stitch. With monofilament thread through the needle and a polyester thread in the bobbin, use a zigzag stitch about 1.5 mm (less than $1/16$ in) long and 1.5 mm (less than $1/16$ in) wide. Gold thread can be used through the needle to couch some of the finer threads.

To couch threads only to the quilt top, begin by knotting the thread to be couched underneath and bringing it up through the fabric with a tapestry needle. To finish, thread it through the tapestry needle again, pull the thread through to the back and knot it against the fabric.

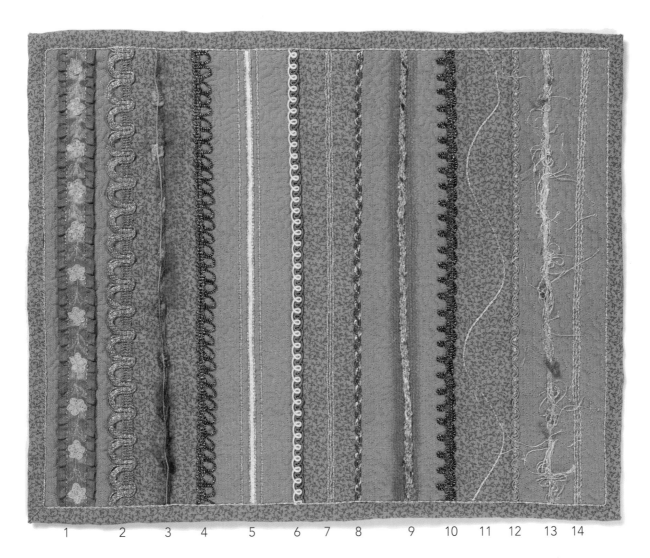

1 2 3 4 5 6 7 8 9 10 11 12 13 14

1: Flowers appliquéd to ribbon with free-machining;
2–14: Use Monofilament or a thread to match the braid and zigzag or free-machine it in place.

Couched threads and fine braids can also be attached after the quilting is completed. To start, use a tapestry needle to insert the thread into the batting layer. Push the needle through the quilt top and into the batting layer without catching the backing. Bring the needle out about 2.5 cm (1 in) from where you will begin stitching. Leave a short tail of thread hanging out. To finish, thread the tapestry needle, insert the needle at the end of the last stitch and bring it out about 2.5 cm (1 in) away from the stitching. Cut the tails level with the top of the quilt and they will pull into the batting out of sight.

Heavy threads and braids that are attached after quilting need to have their raw ends doubled under or overlapped and secured on the top of the quilt with invisible stitches. Have as few joins as possible.

Decorative and textured wools can be used for stems or other embellishments. Unless they are very thick they can be brought through from the back with a tapestry needle to begin and end. Usually it is easiest to use a braiding foot but sometimes a darning foot works just as well. Set the machine for free-machining and, using a narrow zigzag stitch, guide the thread into position with a satay stick as you stitch over it.

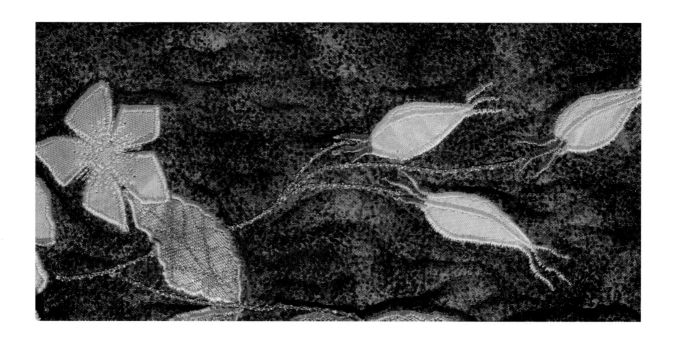

Mythical Beasts Weave Magical Stories detail. Thick gold thread is couched with fine metallic thread to make stems.

Trees and Grasses

1   Cut out the trunks and bunches of leaves. Use a number or letter to distinguish each bunch of leaves.

2   Fuse the main trunk and small branches in place. Extra small branches can be added either with small pieces of tree trunk fabric satin-stitched on top of the leaves or with satin-stitching alone.

3   Satin-stitch the trunks, then fuse the bunches of leaves in place. Free-machine around each bunch of leaves twice.

4   When quilting, outline the bunches of leaves and they will stand out against the background.

5   The small trees have free-machined trunks. Variegated thread works well for these.

Tree tops are made by free-machining over fabric shapes.

Dance of the Brolgas detail. Gum trees.

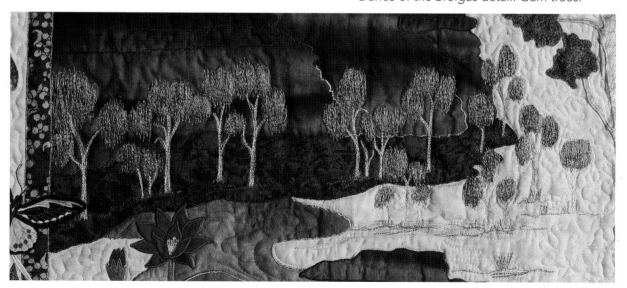

Dance of the Brolgas detail. Free-machined gum trees

Gum trees

1. Satin-stitch the tree trunk. Free-machine twice around bunches of leaves.

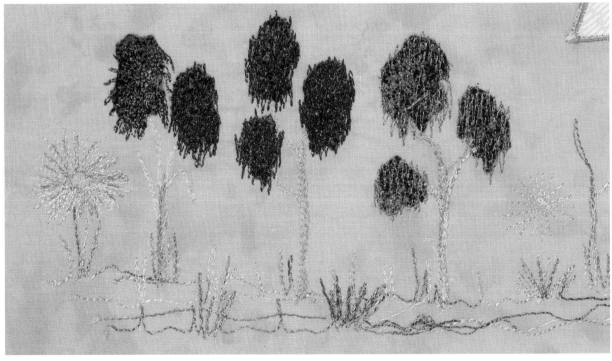

2. Free-machine the trunk with variegated thread and over fabric bunches of leaves with green thread.

Gum trees

Gum tree pattern.

Palm trees

Left side fronds are stitched with extra stitching lines to give a fuller effect.

1   Cut out all the pieces of the tree. Cut the palm fronds in the broad shape as in the diagram. Use a number or letter to distinguish the fronds. Using two different green fabrics can look very effective.

2   Draw a centre line on the tracing paper side of the frond. It is also helpful to indicate the direction of the cuts that will make the frond spikes.

3   Cut spikes up to this line to resemble palm fronds. Make sure you do not cut in too far or the frond will fall apart.

4   Peel away the backing on the trunks and the sand. Fuse them in place and satin-stitch.

5   Carefully peel away the backing from the palm fronds and fuse them in position.

6   Free-machine, stitching over each frond at least once but also adding extra fronds with the stitching.

Marnie's Seagulls Visit the Reef detail.

Palm tree pattern.

Tree ferns and bracken

The palm tree technique can also be used for tree ferns and bracken by altering the basic shape of the leaves, then proceeding as above.

For tree ferns a different-shaped trunk is needed. Tree ferns are shorter and the trunks are much rougher in texture.

Bracken fern often looks like a mass of fronds together so try using various sizes of smaller fronds.

Gold Amongst the Mountain Ash detail. Tree ferns.

Grass trees

1   Cut out the trunks and the light brown under-leaves and fuse them in place. Satin-stitch the trunks and free-machine the under-leaves.

2   Cut out circles of green fabric and then cut out spiky leaves. Draw a guide on the tracing paper to help get the direction of the leaves right.

3   Fuse the leaves in place and free-machine, catching down each spike with at least one line of stitching but at the same time adding extra spikes.

4   Lastly add the flower spikes and free-machine them in place.

The completed grass tree.

Dance of the Brolgas detail. Grass tree.

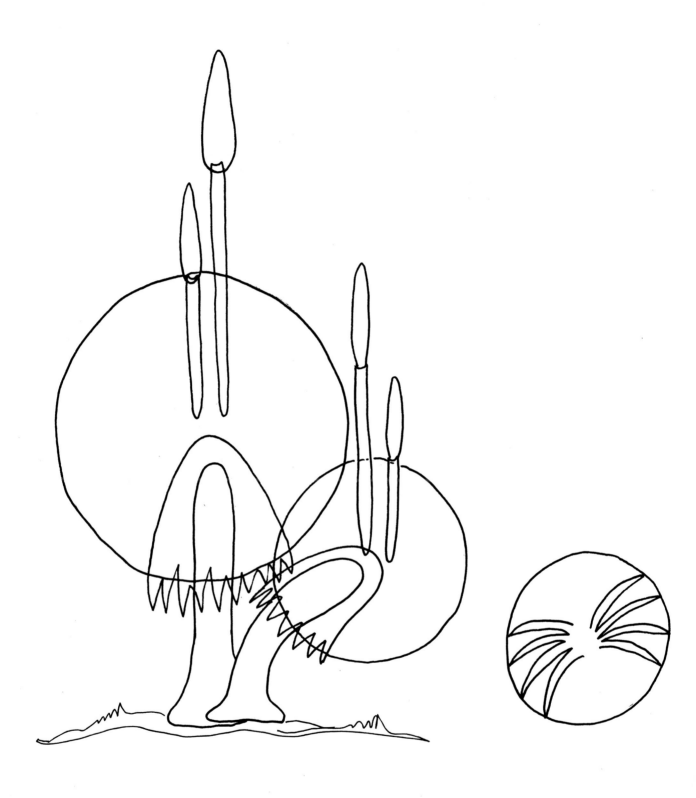

Grass tree pattern
Directions for cutting the circles.

Fantasy trees and more

1 Cut out the trunk and satin-stitch it in place.

2 To make leaves for a tree approximately the size of this page you will need some fabric about 15 cm (6 in) square. Back the leaf fabric with fusible webbing. When it has cooled, peel the backing paper away.

3 Using small sharp scissors, cut leaves in roughly pointed oval shapes from the fabric.

4 Arrange the leaves on the tree branches. I suggest using tweezers to pick up the leaves, as it makes precise placement easier.

5 There will always be some leaves that are upside-down (sticky side up), so place an appliqué mat over the tree before fusing the leaves in place. Peel any leaves off the appliqué mat, turn them over and replace them on the tree, and fuse in position.

6 Free-machine over the leaves, 'drawing' others with the thread as you stitch.

Use one leaf fabric, or two or more, depending on the effect required. It can be very effective to use plain and patterned fabrics together. This gives you more variation with shading and depth of colour. Cutting different sized leaves and arranging them in bunches or spreading them out will also give you many variations. Shades of yellows, reds and browns will give autumn foliage.

Flowers can be added in different colours and shapes.

The same technique can be used for flowering trees. Fabrics in blue shades make good jacaranda trees, pinks and whites for tulip magnolias.

Look at photographs of the tree you are trying to construct and position bunches of leaves or flowers accordingly.

Fantasy tree showing some possible combinations of fabrics and threads.

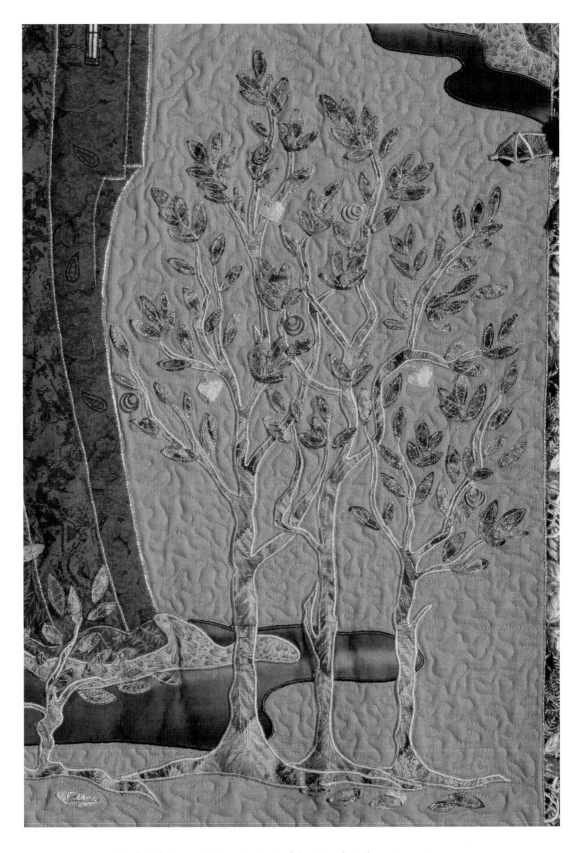

Mythical Beasts Weave Magical Stories detail. Fantasy trees.

Fantasy tree pattern.

Mangroves

Mangrove trees can also be made using small cut-out leaves. It is the trunks that are different and of course they emerge from water.

1 Cut out the water and mangrove trunks. Fuse them in place and satin-stitch.

2 Cut out the leaves. They can be all in the one fabric or a combination of fabrics.

3 Stitch over the leaves with a continuous line of free-machining.

Use a variety of fabrics for the leaves.

Mangrove pattern.

Marnie's Seagulls Visit the Reef detail. Mangroves.

She-oaks

Cut the trunk and branches using the Vliesofix technique. Use a heavy cotton thread or number 30 weight machine embroidery rayon to free-machine the fine feathery leaves.

Marnie's Seagulls Visit the Reef detail. She-oaks.

Grasses

There are many ways to stitch grasses; here are a few suggestions.

★ They can be free-machined with or without small coloured circles to represent flowers.

★ Use fabric paint or Fabrico textile markers to suggest ground and grass, then free-machine over it as above.

★ Use the Vliesofix technique and cut out strips of grass, then free-machine over the top. You can also add seed heads in fabric and as you stitch in the grass include and embellish the seed heads.

Stitched grass over a painted background.

Pelican Twilight detail. Stitched grass over fabric grass and seed-head shapes.

Creatures Small and Large

Using the built-in decorative stitch settings on the machine you can create many small creatures.

★ Join up a line of satin-stitch dots, add some free-machined wings in white or silver thread and you have a dragonfly.

★ One larger satin-stitch dot with four free-machined legs on either side and a couple of eyes make a spider.

★ Make a continuous line of satin-stitching with a bend in the middle; add 'legs' at each end and you have a looper grub.

★ Ants can be stitched with three teardrop-shaped satin-stitch motifs and legs and feelers added with free-machining.

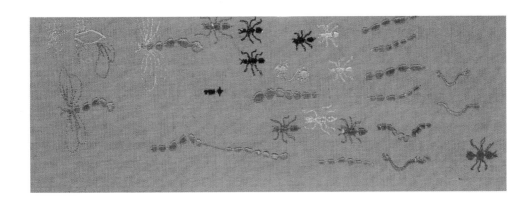

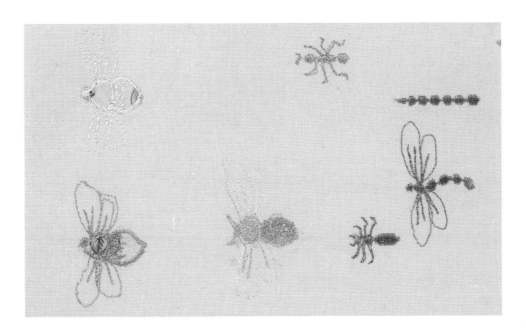

Use built-in machine stitches with a little free-machining for the details.

Butterflies and moths

Butterflies and moths can be made in many different ways.

★ Design your own or use the broderie perse method and stitch them directly on to the background. The bodies can be another piece of fabric attached with Vliesofix or satin-stitched. Begin the stitching with a width of 0; gradually increase the width for the body then decrease again to finish. Add feelers by free-machining.

★ As above, but follow the 3D instructions. Depending on the size of the butterfly, leave the wings free or angle them a little and catch the wing tips down with a few stitches. Velvet or fur fabrics (which sometimes need a 'hair cut'), make effective bodies for these butterflies.

★ Make them from silk 'paper' (see page 89).

★ Butterflies can be decorated with embroidery, beads, foil or Shiva Paintstiks.

★ Make very delicate wings from heat-vanishing muslin or Solvy.

3D butterflies with satin-stitched bodies.

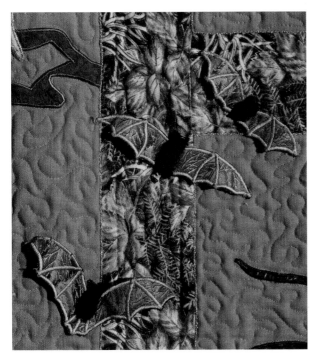

Mythical Beasts Weave Magical Stories detail. The bats have fur fabric bodies with wings attached only at the tips.

Dragonflies

Following the heat-vanishing muslin instructions, draw some wings on heat-vanishing muslin and stitch over them in a lacy pattern.

Use a fabric or satin stitch for the bodies and add a couple of seed beads for the eyes.

Flowers, dragonfly and bees with heat-vanishing muslin petals and wings.

Bees

Bees can be made with fabric bodies and heat-vanishing muslin wings (as described above), or with free-machined wings in white, silver or gold thread.

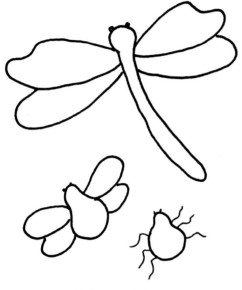

Dragonfly, bee and bug patterns.

Bees with fabric bodies and stitched wings.

Fish

Follow the instructions for 3D padded appliqués. Leave the fins and tail free as you stitch the fish to the background.

Combine a padded appliqué with some heat-vanishing muslin fins. The lower fin can be attached as the satin stitch is done. The second fin is attached over the top later. Add a rhinestone eye.

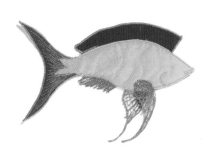

A 3D fairy basslet fish with heat-vanishing muslin fins.

The fish attached to the background with extra padding under the body.

Long-tailed banner fish—padded body with the tail left free.

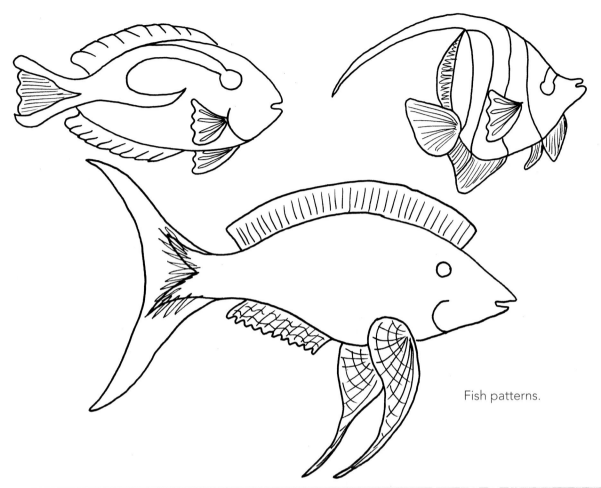

Fish patterns.

Marnie's Seagulls Visit the Reef detail. Padded fish with fins and tails not attached to the background.

Birds

Birds can also be made as 3D padded appliqués. If the wings are spread, either leave them free or angle them slightly and just catch them down at the tips.

Satin-stitching small feathers can be very fiddly, but there is a way of doing it that is easier than stopping and turning very tricky ends. With the feed-dogs still up, stitch to the end of the first feather. Hold your work firmly on either side of the needle then, as you stitch, pull your work sideways, that is, against where the machine would normally feed the fabric. Then pull it the opposite way to come back to the next feather. The stitches will have a different look as they will have gone sideways. It takes a little practice but works really well.

Marnie's Seagulls Visit the Reef detail. Padded seagull with wings attached at the tip.

A Flash of Lorikeets detail. The feather stitching on the birds bodies was done in the method described above.

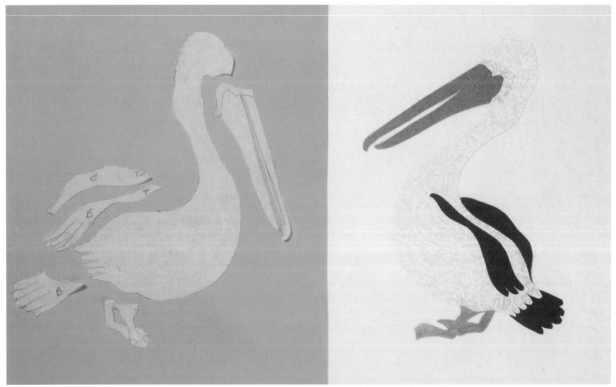

Parts of a pelican and how they fit together.

Pelican patterns.

3D padded dragon

1   Prepare a 'sandwich' following the instructions for 3D appliqué (page 33).

2   Fuse the dragon pieces on top of the Pellon layer using an appliqué mat under the iron.

3   Complete all the satin-stitching and free-machined lines that form the scales on the chest.

4   Carefully cut out the dragon. If you snip a stitch by mistake, use some Fray-Stop or craft glue on the end of a toothpick to hold the snipped stitches in place.

Dragon assembled on a 'sandwich' of backing fabric—two layers of iron-on Vilene and one layer of Pellon on a backing fabric.

Stitch the dragon then cut it out.

Dragon pattern.

Medieval Inspirations detail. A 3D dragon

Flowers

Chrysanthemums

1 Trace all three layers of the flower separately onto Vliesofix, fuse each to the flower fabric and cut out.

2 The largest layer is fused directly to the background fabric and stitched.

3 Prepare a base 'sandwich' as for 3D appliqués.

4 Fuse the middle and top layers of the chrysanthemum on to the top layer of the iron-on Vilene and free-machine all the petals, stitching twice around to define them.

5 Cut out the shapes.

6 Cut a hole in the centre of the middle layer. When the middle and top layers are attached you will be stitching only through the top layer.

Middle and top layers on a 'sandwich'.

Stitch both pieces and cut a hole on the middle layer.

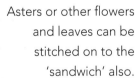

Asters or other flowers and leaves can be stitched on to the 'sandwich' also.

The bottom layer is stitched directly on to the background. The middle layer is held by stitching through the top layer.

Chrysanthemum pattern.
Trace each layer separately.

Iron Lace—Autumn detail. Chrysanthemums and asters.

Iris

These beautiful flowers can either be fused and stitched directly to the background or put onto a 'sandwich' of stabiliser and made into 3D flowers.

For 3D flowers, first stitch, then cut them out. Fuse the top of the stem to the base of the flower and satin-stitch the stem and the very base of the iris onto the background fabric. Leave the rest of the iris free until the quilting has been completed. Lastly, attach the tips of the petals to the background, allowing the flower to stand away slightly.

Iris patterns.

Attach the tips of the iris flowers after the background has been quilted.

Iron Lace—Spring detail. Iris, some attached directly to the background, some after quilting.

Flowers with many petals

Flowers such as iris, roses, peonies or chrysanthemums that you are intending to stitch directly to the background can be cut in one piece and the petals defined with satin-stitching. Use a thread either lighter or darker in colour that will contrast a little with the flower fabric. Begin by stitching the petals at the back of the flower and move forward.

Iron Lace—Spring detail. Roses, tulips and daffodils with petals defined by stitching.

Rose pattern.

Happy Wanderer (hardenbergia)

Happy Wanderer can be very fiddly to make by the 3D technique because the flowers are so small. Instead of trying to cut each one out and stitch it, it is better to cover the stabiliser 'sandwich' with purple fabric, and stitch the flowers over a guide drawn with a dressmaker's pencil or other light-coloured marker. Make the flowers in about three different sizes so that you have a gradation in size along each spray. Cut them out and attach them to the background by stitching in the stamens with yellow thread. Their leaves can be three-dimensional too. Make the winding creeper stems using couched textured wool.

Happy Wanderer (hardenbergia) flower and leaf patterns.

Stitch the flowers on a 'sandwich'.

Iron Lace—Winter detail. Happy Wanderer (hardenbergia) over iron lace.

Cherry blossom

Put some pale pink fabric into a hoop. Free-machine the outline of a blossom shape with dark pink thread, using the same thread in the bobbin. Stitch over this shape again. Move to another spot in the hoop and stitch another blossom. Repeat as many times as you need, moving the fabric in the hoop as necessary.

Remove the hoop. You will find that the blossoms curl up a little, which is the effect that you want.

Use a light red or pale pink Aquarelle or Derwent Inktense pencil to colour the blossoms from the centres towards the edges (but not all the way). With a damp cloth 'blush' the pencil marks. Cut out the blossoms.

Use a darker red or pink thread to attach each flower, starting in the centre and stitching the stamens to hold it in place. Use a yellow pencil to highlight the flower centre.

These cherry blossoms are best used on a project that will not be washed, as it is difficult to heat-set the pencil colours on the curled flower surface.

1. Stitch blossoms in a hoop.

2. Colour the centres and cut out the blossoms. Attach them using a darker pink/red for the stamens and finish with a yellow centre, as shown in the detail from *Iron Lace—Spring.*

Iron Lace—Spring detail. Cherry blossoms

Silk flowers

Put silk or a synthetic fabric firmly into a hoop and use the cherry blossom technique to make small flowers. They will curl up beautifully when released and stitched in place and look very effective among larger flowers or even in a group by themselves.

Small Silk Flowers

1. Put silk or other fine fabric into a hoop.
2. Stitch flower shapes using free-machining technique. Stitch around each shape twice.
3. Remove from hoop and cut out flowers.
4. Attach to background by free-machining the stamens.

1. Stitch flower shapes in a hoop.

2. Cut them out and attach them by stitching the stamens. Add beads or rhinestones.

Gum blossom

Gum blossoms are free-machined, not cut from fabric.

To begin, using gold metallic thread, stitch a small circle for the centre of the flower and then 'spikes' radiating out from the circle all the way round. Change to red thread and stitch over the gold. Some red will cover the gold, some will not. The idea is to have the gold shine through from underneath, giving a sparkle to the flower. A little T-shaped stitching across the centre circle finishes the blossom.

Combinations of gold and yellow or silver and white also work well.

For extra sparkle or accent, either stitch seed beads around the edge of the blossoms or glue on tiny fingernail rhinestones.

Step 1: Use gold thread to stitch the basic shape.

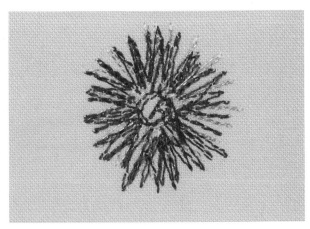

Step 2: Use red thread over the top.

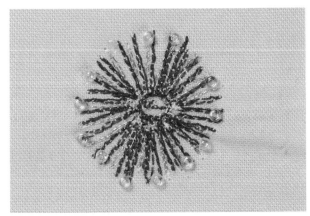

Step 3: Add beads or rhinestones to the edges.

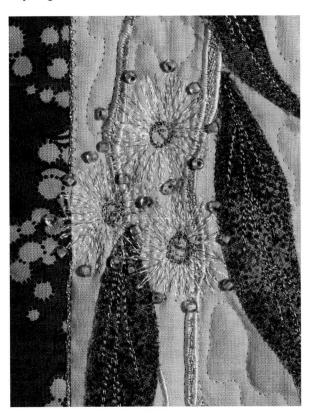

Dance of the Brolgas detail. Beads have been stitched round the edges of the gum blossoms.

Combining flowers

An urn of flowers using basic appliqué and the 3D methods look very effective.

Cut the urn from one piece of fabric and stitch the details with satin stitch.

The flower urn

Detail from *Iron Lace - Spring* showing urn filled with a combination of flowers.

Wattle blossom and leaves

Wattle blossoms are made by stitching 'across space' over holes that have been cut in fabric held in a hoop.

Set up the sewing machine for free-machining. Use yellow thread in the top and the bobbin as both threads will be seen. It can be the same yellow but two different yellow shades also look good.

Use an 18 cm (7 in) diameter plastic and metal spring hoop or wooden hoop.

Put a piece of calico or light-coloured scrap fabric to be used as the base for the blossoms into the hoop, making sure that the fabric is tightly stretched. Cut out one circle about 2 cm (¾ in) in diameter.

Put the needle into the fabric near the edge of the hole and bring up the bobbin thread.

Hold top and bobbin threads together and begin to stitch 'across space' to the opposite side of the hole and into the fabric again. Stitch a couple of stitches into the fabric, moving around the hole a little, then across the hole again to the opposite side, crossing the first line of stitching in the centre. It will look like the spokes on a bicycle wheel. Continue in this manner until you have a blossom which is attached to the hole by its edges. It is very important to keep crossing in the centre. If you don't do this, you will not have any thread to fluff up on the edge of the blossom.

If it becomes too difficult because of thread build-up to stitch across the centre, either hold the presser foot up slightly while stitching across or, instead of stitching all the way, stitch nearly to the centre, then out to the edge, continuing all the way round in the same manner.

Do not cut out the finished the blossom yet, as tension will be lost on the hoop. Cut another hole, make another blossom and continue. Make a few different-sized blossoms by varying the diameter of the holes. When the hoop is full, move the hoop along the fabric and continue until you have as many blossoms as you want.

Each blossom can then be cut against the calico edge. Attach them to your project with a few free-machine stitches through the centres. They can be fluffed up by rubbing your finger over them.

Wattle leaves

Some wattle leaves are very fine and lie in clusters along a stem. Instead of cutting many small pieces that have to be put in place individually, cut the leaves as a group, leaving a fine 'stem' of fabric through the centre. This can be cut away after the leaves have been fused in place. Just ease the bits of stem off the fabric with a pin or the point of your scissors and cut it off. Alternatively it can be stitched over if it is not too thick.

Free-machine the fused leaves and add the stem again, either with free-machining or a fine satin-stitch. This works well for other leaves with multiple leaflets.

Wattle leaves pattern. Cut these all in one piece.

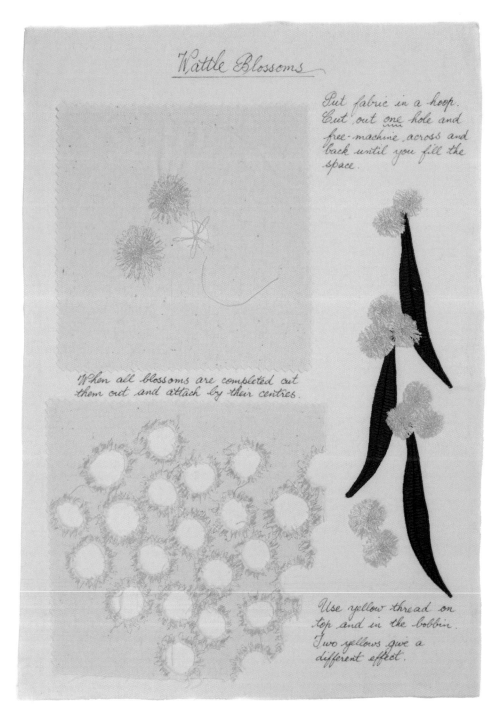

Wattle Blossoms

Put fabric in a hoop. Cut out one hole and free-machine across and back until you fill the space.

When all blossoms are completed cut them out and attach by their centres.

Use yellow thread on top and in the bobbin. Two yellows give a different effect.

1. Cut one hole at a time and stitch across it.

2. Cut out the blossoms.

3. Stitch the leaves in place first, then add the blossoms.

Variation: Bottlebrush

To make bottlebrush flowers, cut a rectangular hole and stitch two or three rows between the short sides of the rectangle in the centre of the hole. Then, stitch back and forth between the short sides. When this piece is cut out you will have a bottlebrush shape.

Wattle blossom cushion, detail.

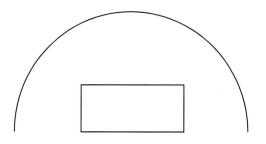

Step 1. Cut a rectangle in the hoop

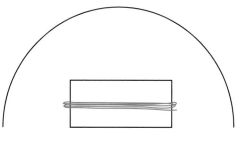

Step 2. Use red thread. Stitch across and back a few times between the long sides.

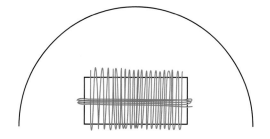

Step 3. Stitch across and back between the short sides until the space is filled.

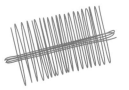

Step 4. Cut the stitching close to the support fabric.

To make bottlebrush flowers.

Buildings and Iron Lace

Buildings

Representing buildings in fabric appliqué can be great fun.

1   First you must have a sharp, preferably colour, photograph of the building. Starting with a 15 x 23 cm (6 x 9 in) photograph is ideal, but a smaller one will do. Using a photocopier make a black and white copy in the size that you want your finished appliqué.

2   A light table is excellent for this next step, but you can also hold your photocopy up to a window. Trace over the main lines of the building. Use tracing or parchment paper so that you can simply use the reverse side as the pattern side. Do mark 'right side' so you don't get confused. What you are doing here is defining the areas you will need to cut out of different fabrics. Some of the detail you will be able to put in with satin-stitching or free-machining later.

3   Trace the pieces from the reverse side of your drawing onto Vliesofix. Make sure you include underlaps as you go. Mark them on your original tracing to be sure. Refer to the colour photograph if you want your building to look 'real'.

4   Cut out the pieces and assemble them either directly on the background or first on an appliqué mat so that you can handle them as a whole unit. Fuse the building in place.

5   Complete the stitching, adding building details, a garden, fence or street scene to finish.

Photograph the building.

Make a photocopy in the finished size.

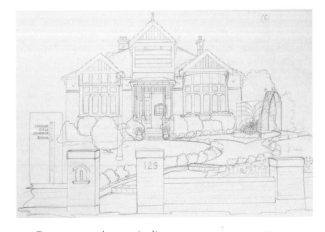

Draw over the main lines to get your pattern.

The appliquéd and quilted result.

Iron lace

To stitch an iron lace design, follow steps 1 and 2 above, except in this case you will have only one fabric. Iron lace looks lovely when cut out of a colour-on-colour patterned fabric.

Cut the main part out of a single piece of fabric. If there are many identical pieces that hang from the lower edge for example, it is sometimes easier to cut these separately and fuse them on after you have got the main area in place.

Use a narrow satin stitch to outline the 'lace' and to define any flowers or motifs within the design.

Iron Lace—Winter detail. The triangular section is cut all in one piece

Making Silk Paper

Making silk paper butterflies

For making silk paper you will need:

★ plastic sheet to cover work area

★ net, 2 pieces each about 50 cm (20 in) square, for each 'paper' you make. These are used as a support while the 'paper' is being made and are re-usable in the next paper-making session.

★ 2 cheap household paint brushes 5–8 cm (2–3 in) wide

★ Jo Sonja Textile Medium

★ washing-up liquid (a few drops)

★ containers for water—ice-cream or yoghurt containers are ideal

★ mopping-up cloths

★ silk tops

Note: A silk top is made of strands of silk that have been carded and combed to align the fibres. Silk tops come in a range of beautifully dyed colours. One 25 g silk top will make one or two sheets of medium thick silk paper about 30 x 40 cm (12 x 18 in), depending on how thickly the fibres are laid down.

Place one piece of net on the plastic sheet. The net should be 7–10 cm (3–4 in) larger all round than the silk paper you are making.

The silk is layered onto the net. You can have one, two or three layers depending on the purpose of the silk paper.

First, separate a manageable length of silk from the top. Then, hold the end of the silk in one hand and with the other hand hold it about 15 cm (5–6 in) away. Pull gently on the silk and a length of fibres will come away easily. Layer these fibres vertically on the net. Continue in this manner until you have completed one layer.

A second layer should be placed at right angles to the first layer. A third layer will be at right angles to the second layer, that is, the same direction as the first layer. Three thin layers will be stronger in all directions than two thick layers.

Because both sides of the finished paper will be the 'right' side you can have different colours on the first and last layers. If you have three layers, the middle layer shows least colour so that you can 'hide' a colour there (save your favourite colours for the outsides) although you may still see some of it. You can also trap things such as threads, decorative wools, small pieces of fabric, Angelina fibre (the standard type works best; see page 93), glitter or flakes within the silk fibres. If the layers are thin these will show through even if you put them between layers. Use them sparingly as it is the silk that should be the star! When you have made one or two sheets you will be able to judge how thick the paper must be for your purpose and whether, or how much, glitter gives the look that you want.

Use the second piece of net to cover the layered silk. Using one of the brushes paint *both sides* with a solution of soapy water—approximately 1 teaspoon of detergent to 300 ml (10 ½ fl oz) of water. It is very important to make sure that you work the soapy water thoroughly into the silk. This will allow the Textile Medium to penetrate the fibres thoroughly. Wipe up the excess soapsuds.

Paint on the Textile Medium (follow manufacturer's instructions), using the second brush. Work the Textile Medium well into the silk. Again, paint both sides. The layers will separate if the liquid has not penetrated properly.

Dry with the net still in place, ideally lying flat on a frame. A cake cooling rack can be used for small pieces. If this is not possible, then hang it on a line out of the sun (peg the net, not the paper). You can also use a hairdryer but that will make the paper quite stiff. Whichever way you dry it, it will drip colour, so make sure that there is something to catch the drips.

Note: Never leave the silk paper lying on the plastic sheeting to dry, as it will become shiny from the Textile Medium remaining on the plastic.

When the paper is perfectly dry, carefully remove the net. Test a corner first—if the net is still sticking, leave it to dry a little longer. When you remove the net, peel it away in the direction of the last layer of silk that was laid down. The net can be washed and re-used.

Iron the paper to smooth out any wrinkles. Use a medium heat setting with a press cloth, or put the 'paper' between two sheets of brown paper. Pressing the 'paper' sets the Textile Medium and also makes it water repellent.

The finished silk paper can be used for appliqué, stitched, beaded or embellished in many ways.

1. Vliesofix a butterfly design to fabric and cut it out.

2. Fuse butterfly on to the 'sandwich' and embroider it.

3. Cut the finished butterfly. Use the body to attach it to the background.

Butterfly patterns.

Across Dark Roads to Freedom detail. Butterflies embroidered and embellished.

Embellishing Backgrounds and Appliqués

Foils

Foils are thin layers of metallic plastic that have been attached to cellophane. They come in a range of beautiful colours, both plain and multicoloured.

They can be used at any stage of a project—on the background fabric, on the appliqués either before or after they are attached, or as one of the last processes to enhance the design before quilting.

Glue is applied to the background fabric or the appliqué allowed to dry and then the foil is ironed on.

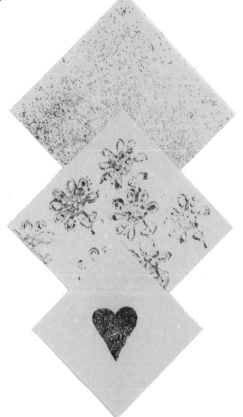

Top—foil applied over sprinkled bonding powder.
Centre—glue painted on a wooden block, stamped and foil applied.
Bottom—foil over a Vliesofixed shape

Applying the glue

This can be done in a number of ways.

★ Use a clear-drying flexible glue (Jones Tones Plexi Glue or similar) to draw a design directly onto the fabric.

★ Use a paintbrush or foam roller to put the glue onto a rubber stamp or wooden block, then stamp onto the fabric. This does not always transfer perfectly but gives lovely effects.

★ Pour a small amount of glue into a shallow container. Use a toothbrush, comb or sponge to 'draw' on the fabric.

★ Use a bonding powder (such as Audrey's Bond) to sprinkle glue spots on the fabric.

Allow the glue to dry completely (it turns clear). Lay the sheet of foil, colour side up over the dried glue, cover it with baking paper or an appliqué mat and use a fairly hot iron with reasonable pressure. Leave it to cool, then peel away the backing sheet. The foil should have adhered to the fabric over the glued design. There will still be coloured foil left on the sheet and this can be reused until all the colour has gone. It is also possible to iron more colours over the first one.

You can also cut shapes from fusible web and fuse them in position on the fabric, remove the backing paper from the fusible web and apply the foil over your shape as above. This will give you solid foil colours. Another idea is to stitch the fabric with fusible thread (such as Superior Threads' Charlotte's Fusible Web). Use straight stitch, zigzag or other decorative stitches. Place the foil over the top and iron it on following the glue instructions above.

Iris Variations detail. Foil applied to background fabric with appliquéd and quilted flowers over it.

Angelina fibre

Angelina fibre is a very fine, super soft, decorative polyester fibre. There are two types heat-bondable (Hot Fix Angelina) and standard.

Heat-bondable Angelina will only bond to itself. It is very soft to the touch and gives a lovely sparkling effect when added to other fibres. It is washable and dries very quickly.

Place a small amount of fibre between two pieces of baking paper and with your iron on the 'silk' setting move it gently back and forth to fuse the fibres together. The result will be a beautiful, fine non-woven fabric. The fibres should bond quite quickly so check their progress frequently. If the fibres do not bond they may need a little more pressing or maybe a slightly hotter iron. Too much pressing or heat will dull the sparkle so take it slowly. Using a hotter iron will also change some of the colours. Experiment!

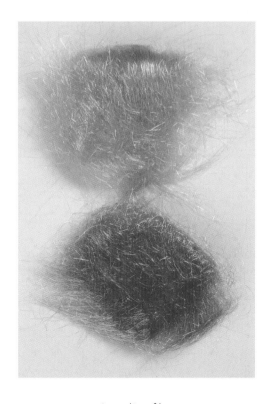

Angelina fibre

You can use just a little of the fibre and make a web-like fabric, or use a lot and make something quite dense and firm. The fibres can be laid down in any direction, straight or swirled. Try blending different colours as well. Pieces of thread, glitter, sequins or standard Angelina can be trapped between the fibres before they are ironed. Often there will be lots of loose fibres left on the outer edges, so if you want a straight edge to the 'fabric', simply turn the loose fibres under and bond again.

Standard Angelina fibres must be placed between hot fix fibres as they will not bond to themselves. They can be used to add a different texture and/or colour to the hot fix 'fabric', as a fine layer between two hot fix layers, or mixed and muddled with the hot fix fibres. They also work well trapped in silk 'paper', giving it sparkle.

Angelina fibre used as appliqué fabric.

Dragon wings made from Angelina fibre.

Angelina 'fabric' must be stitched or glued to the background fabric. Treat it as another fabric and cut appliqués from it. These can be put on using Vliesofix, or machined on directly. Cut edges will not fray.

These hot fix fibres can also be moulded over something like thick lace, a wooden print block or a metal grid. To do this place baking paper over the textured surface, then the Angelina fibres, a second piece of baking paper on top, and iron firmly. You will need to make a fairly solid fabric to get a good impression. Being careful not to move the fibres, you can check if the impression is clear and press again if necessary.

Paintstiks

Paintstiks are made from pigment, oil and wax and look like large crayons wrapped in cardboard tubes. Shiva Paintstiks and Markal Paintstiks are the same product under different names. They come in many colours, including an iridescent range.

Paintstiks are self-healing, so that a skin forms over the crayon when it is not in use. This skin must be peeled away to use the Paintstik. Pinch off the skin using a paper towel, or use a sharp knife. The colour is permanent so take care not to get it on your clothes. The skin keeps the Paintstik from drying out and so they will keep for years.

Being used like a crayon, they are easily applied directly to fabric. You can add layers of different colour as you go.

Paintstiks can be used over a rubbing plate or metal mesh to give different textures. A selection of rubbing plates, from leaves and flowers to geometric designs, is available from Paintstik suppliers. Paintstiks are also good for stencilling. It is best to tape the fabric firmly to your work area when stencilling or using a rubbing plate, otherwise you will not get a clear image.

Leave the work for at least three or four days to dry completely. It is usually touch-dry in 24 hours but it needs to cure. Then the Paintstik colour needs to be heat set. First cover your ironing surface with greaseproof paper to protect it from the oils in the paint. Place your fabric on the paper paint-side down. Set the iron at a temperature appropriate to the fabric. Press (don't iron) each section of the fabric for 10 to 15 seconds. This will make the colour permanent.

Fabrics decorated with Paintstik colours are washable in cold water. Do not dry clean as this will break down the paint.

Gold Amongst the Mountain Ash detail. Paintstiks used to embellish the birds

Party Prawns but who invited the Crab? Paintstiks used to embellish the background.

Chroma Coal Pastels

Chroma Coal heat-fixable pastels can be used on any fabric that will stand being ironed on the cotton setting to set them. They are easy to use and the lighter colours will give a lovely blush of colour to a background.

Fabric paints

There are many brands of fabric paint to choose from. One of the easiest to use is Setacolour. Paint it on, let it dry and then heat-set it with an iron following the manufacturer's instructions.

Moon Shadow Mist Sprays

Moon Shadow Mist Sprays are an 'olde worlde walnut ink' formula in beautiful colours. They come as a powder to which you just add hot water the first time you use them. Instructions come with the product. They are intended for books and mixed media but also work well with fabric.

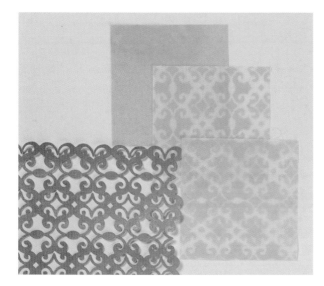

Moon Shadow Mist Spray examples:
Top—all over;
Centre and bottom—over stencils.

Tea-dyeing

If a fabric is not quite the colour you need, over-dyeing with tea or coffee may be the answer. It is best for small quantities of fabric. Different teas will give different colours, ranging from pale old gold through to almost pink shades with some herbal fruit teas. Coffee gives a richer brown colour.

To dye with tea, use two tea bags per cup of water. For a more intense colour use more tea bags or allow the brew to steep longer. Place the tea bags in a container large enough to hold the fabric, pour boiling water over them and allow the tea to brew for 8–10 minutes.

Wet the fabric and squeeze it out before putting it in the dye bath. Let it soak in the tea solution for 10–15 minutes. It will dry a lighter colour than it seems when wet so it may need a longer time.

To dye with coffee, use a heaped teaspoon of granules per cup of hot water. For a darker colour use more coffee or let the fabric soak for a longer time.

When you have the desired colour, squeeze out the fabric and rinse it in tap water. Line-dry it or put it in the dryer with an old towel as some of the colour may come out.

Aquarelle and Derwent Inktense pencils

To achieve a colour-wash effect with these pencils, wet the fabric before applying the colour. For sharper lines, dip just the tips of the pencils in water (do not soak the wood or the pencil will become soggy and break) and draw on dry fabric. For something between the two, use the pencils dry, directly on the fabric, then use a small wet paint brush to spread the colour a little. If you want to wash the project, paint over the pencilled areas with a thin layer of Jo Sonja's Textile Medium.

Stamps and stencils

Stamps and stencils are very useful for creating backgrounds for appliqués. Wooden stamps are excellent for using with foil. Paint glue onto the stamp, stamp the fabric, allow it to dry, then apply the foil (see page 92). There are also lovely designs in rubber and foam stamps that can be used in the same way. Angelina fibre can be used over wooden stamps to give beautiful textured impressions (see page 92).

Stencils come in plastic or heavy card. Many can be found with supplies for scrap-booking and paperwork. They can be used with sprays, fabric paint or any other appropriate fabric colour.

Rhinestones and goggle-eyes bring creatures to life

Rhinestones, goggle-eyes and trinkets

Rhinestones come in many sizes and colours. They bring life to birds and creatures when they are used as eyes, and can add a bit of glitz in many projects. Goggle-eyes are excellent for novelty projects, but do not use them on quilts for very small children.

Some rhinestones have glue already on them (the hot-fix variety) and are attached with a hot-fix wand that can be purchased for this purpose. It

has different sizes of tips for the different sizes of rhinestones.

Other rhinestones and the goggle-eyes do not have glue already on them. They can be attached with Helmar Gemstone glue, You Can Wash It craft glue or something similar that will dry clear. Use a toothpick and put the glue on the fabric where you want the rhinestone. It is easy to pick up the rhinestone with a tiny amount of glue on the other end of the toothpick. You need enough glue on the fabric that it will just come up the side of the stone slightly to hold it firmly in place. Leave it to dry thoroughly.

Little trinkets often add a sparkle. These usually have a small hole somewhere and can be stitched on by hand after the quilting has been completed.

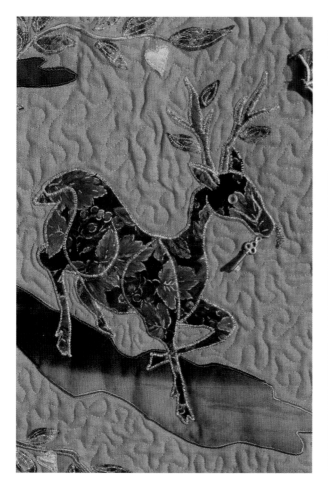

Mythical Beasts Weave Magical Stories details. Trinkets and buttons embellish trees.

Real flowers fabric

Using real flowers is a fun way to decorate a fabric project that will not be washed and is not meant to last indefinitely. It could be used as a decoration or for an Artist Trading Card. The same technique can be used on paper with or without the stitching.

Choose flowers with petals that are reasonably soft and will lie flat. Some flowers such as daisies can be pulled apart.

You will need:

★ Fresh flowers

★ Fusible Web 606 spray adhesive (or Vliesofix)

★ Iron-on stabiliser

★ Background fabric (or paper)

Hydrangea, rose, poppy, marigold petals and callistemon flowers fused to fabric.

Method 1

Fuse an iron-on stabiliser to the back of the fabric before you begin if the flowers are to be stitched over later.

Spray the right side of the fabric with Fusible Web 606 spray adhesive. You will need to protect the area around your work and work in a well-ventilated space.

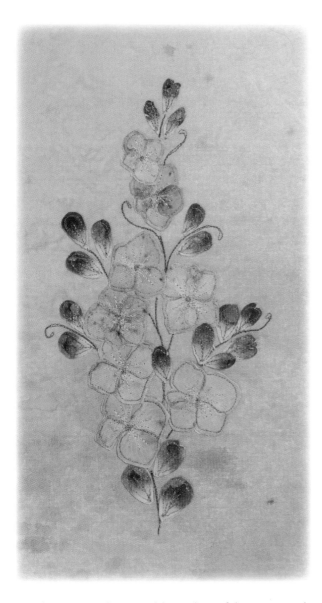

Hydrangea and marigold petals on fabric sprayed with Moon Glow Mist.

Arrange the flowers or petals on the sprayed surface. Spray again so that the flowers are trapped between the layers of adhesive.

Once the adhesive has dried thoroughly (allow 24 hours), you can embellish the flowers with stitching.

Method 2

If you cannot obtain the 606 spray, Vliesofix can be used. This works well except that the Vliesofix leaves a noticeable residue, especially on darker fabrics. If you cut out the flowers and treat them as appliqués this is not as obvious.

Back the background fabric with an iron-on stabiliser so that you will not have Vliesofix sticking to the ironing board later. You will not be able to turn your work face-down to iron a backing onto it once it is covered with Vliesofix!

Cut a piece of Vliesofix the size of the background fabric and fuse it in place on the right side of the fabric. Allow to cool, then remove the paper backing.

Arrange the flowers or petals on the background fabric and cover them with another piece of Vliesofix. Fuse this in place, trapping the petals underneath.

Allow to cool, then remove the paper backing.

Now you can embellish the flowers with stitching. I have some sample pieces that are now over two years old and although the colour has faded somewhat they are still in good condition.

Making tassels

Tassels can be made on the sewing machine. This means that you can always have tassels of any size that match the colours of your project.

You will need a piece of firm card approximately 6 x 12 cm (2 ½ x 5 in) and your chosen colour machine thread. Rayons look lovely and mixing in a metallic thread will give a bit of sparkle.

Use a craft knife to cut a rectangular hole in the centre of the card. It should be twice the length of the finished tassel and about 2.5 cm (1 in) wide.

On the long sides, mark the centre of the hole and about 1 cm (½ in) either side of that mark (see diagram). This will be the head of the tassel.

Cut a small nick in the top of the card to hold the ends of the thread.

2. A selection of tassels made with rayon and metallic threads.

1. Broderie perse fans with tassels.

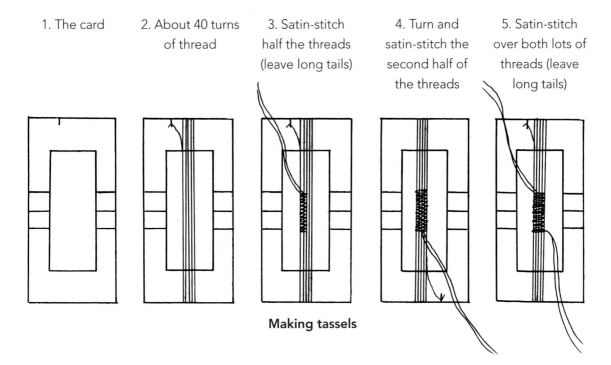

1. The card   2. About 40 turns of thread   3. Satin-stitch half the threads (leave long tails)   4. Turn and satin-stitch the second half of the threads   5. Satin-stitch over both lots of threads (leave long tails)

Making tassels

Anchor the end of the thread in one of the small cuts and begin winding the thread around the card. This can be a single thread, two or three colours, or a colour and a metallic thread. Keep the threads towards the centre of the card as you will be stitching over them. If you are using more than one thread, wind them together and use fewer turns. Anchor the end of the thread.

You will need about 40 turns of thread, depending on how thick you want the tassel.

Thread the machine with the same colour thread on top and in the bobbin and use the satin-stitch setting.

Place the card under the machine. Pull out about 30 cm (12 in) of both the top and bobbin threads and keep them out of the way of the stitching.

Use a zigzag stitch that will cover half of the wound threads and begin stitching from the first of the marks in the centre of the card to the third mark.

Turn the card around, keeping the long beginning threads out of the way, and zigzag-stitch over the other half of the wound threads.

Turn the card again and now zigzag over all the threads.

Pull out another 30 cm (12 in) of top and bobbin threads and cut them off.

Snip across the threads at the top and bottom of the card to release the tassel.

Fold the tassel in half.

Wind one pair of the 30 cm (12 in) threads clockwise and the other pair anti-clockwise around the head of the tassel to form the neck.

Tie the ends in a knot, then thread them into a needle and bury them in the neck of the tassel.

Machine Quilting

For machine quilting, prepare your backing, which should be 5 cm (2 in) bigger all round than the quilt top. Lay it out wrong side up on a smooth flat surface, such as a large table or the floor (banish cats, dogs and children first). Pull the edges of the backing taut, but do not stretch them, and tape down the corners and side-centres with masking tape. Use a couple more pieces of tape on each side for a large piece. Place the batting, which should be the same size as the backing, on the backing and smooth it out. If you have to join pieces of batting, butt the edges together and sew them with a diagonal basting stitch. Do not overlap them or you will have a ridge in the finished quilt. A hairdryer helps to remove fold marks and fluff up the batting. Tape the batting into position, then place your thoroughly pressed quilt top, right side up, on top of the batting, making sure that the centres of the quilt top edges line up with the centre points on the edges of the backing. Tape the quilt top in place.

Beginning at the centre of one edge and working to one corner, then working from the centre edge again to the other corner, put in 2.5 cm (1 in) safety pins, about 5 cm (2 in) apart. Move to the opposite side of the quilt and repeat, and then do the last two sides. You will now have safety pins right round the edge of the quilt.

Working from the edges toward the centre of the quilt, place safety pins 8–10 cm (3–4 in) apart over the entire quilt. For a large quilt you will need about 400–500 pins. Try not to place pins where you intend to stitch—for example, in the ditch on any sashing. Avoid pinning appliqués if at all possible—pin around them. Be very careful when pinning silk as it marks so easily. Pin against appliqués or in a spot that will be covered by quilting. Use the back of a spoon or a round-tipped pate knife to lift the pin as you close it. It is much faster and saves your fingers. Remove the tape and you are ready for quilting. Pinning in this manner and taking out the pins as you go is much easier than pulling basting threads out from under machine quilting.

These four samples are free-machine quilted. Mark the centre of the block and then stitch in a continuous line.

Test colours and ideas for quilting on a sample, as on this sample for *Across Dark Roads to Freedom.*

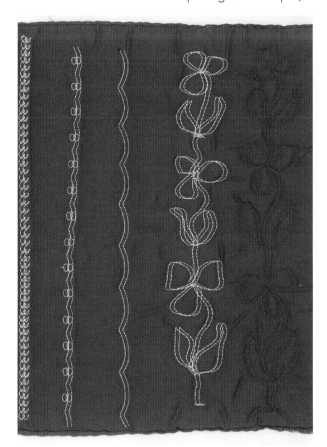

Twin needle patterns can be used for a different effect. (The bobbin thread will be a zigzag.)

Marking the quilt top for quilting

The choice of marker depends on the colour of the fabric and the type of design to be quilted. Always test the marker on a scrap of fabric first to check for visibility and to see how easily the marks can be removed.

Some suggestions for suitable markers are a silver pencil, a fine H lead pencil, a coloured pencil a couple of shades darker than the fabric, tailor's chalk, quilter's tape 6 mm (¼ in) wide, a chalk wheel or a water-soluble blue pen. If you use a water-soluble pen, make sure it is really soluble and wash the quilt thoroughly as soon as possible to remove the marks.

To mark complex patterns such as animals or birds, the easiest way is to trace them onto paper such as Stitch n' Tear or greaseproof paper, using an H or HB pencil. Do not use a very soft lead pencil as the lead tends to mark the quilt as it is stitched. Leave a margin of at least 4 cm (1½ in) all round, then use straight pins to pin it to the area to be quilted. Use at least four pins, one per corner, or more if it is a large design. You can stitch over the tracing very accurately and easily using a darning foot. When you have finished, tear the paper away. Tweezers are very useful for removing the last small scraps of paper. Purchased patterns can also be used.

The pelican has been traced onto paper and stitched. Half the paper is torn away.

Iris Variations detail. The bird has been quilted in two colours of rayon threads. In between, free leaves and flowers are quilted in rayon thread to blend with the background

A Flash of Lorikeets detail. The lorikeets have been quilted with gold thread over paper. The ground between them is filled in with 'free' leaves.

Gallery

Dance of the Brolgas 143 x 141 cm (56 x 55 in)

Tumbling Fans 105 x 126 cm (41 x 50 in)

Reptiles on Centre Stage 161 x 195 cm (63 x 77 in)

Mythical Beasts Weave Magical Stories 200 x 126 cm (79 x 50 in)

Gold Amongst the Mountain Ash 109 x 123 cm (43 x 49 in)

Marnie's Seagulls Visit the Reef 222 x 186 cm (88 x 71 in)

Medieval Inspirations 170 x 210 cm (67 x 83 in)

Across Dark Roads to Freedom 130 x 130 cm (51 x 51 in)

Iron Lace—Summer 150 x 150 cm (59 x 59 in)

Iron Lace—Autumn 150 x 150 cm (59 x 59 in)

Iron Lace—Winter 150 x 150 cm (59 x 59 in)

Iron Lace—Spring 150 x 150 cm (59 x 59 in)

Pelican Twilight 190 x 170 cm (75 x 67 in)

A Flash of Lorikeets 130 x 130 cm (51 x 51 in)

Iris Variations 130 x 130 cm (51 x 51 in)

A Final Word

There are many ways to appliqué fabrics together and an enormous range of decorative possibilities to choose from. Hopefully you have been inspired to try at least something in this book.

Use it as a starting point and adapt ideas to suit your own designs. Above all, enjoy whatever you do to create wonderful appliquéd projects.

Resources

Books

Jane Dunnewold, *Complex Cloth*, Fibre Studio Press, 1996

Alysn Midgelow-Marsden, *Between the Sheets with Angelina*, Word4word, 2003

Maurine Noble & Elizabeth Hendricks, *Machine Quilting with Decorative Threads*, That Patchwork Place, 1998

Judith Pinnell, *Take Silk*, Sally Milner Publishing, 2001

Shelly Stokes, *Paintstiks on Fabric*, Cedar Canyon Textiles, 2005

Terry White, *Thread Painting Made Easy*, American Quilters' Society, 2008

Suppliers

General
The Thread Studio
6 Smith Street
Perth, Western Australia 6000
Phone: 08 9227 1561
International: +61 8 9227 1561
www.thethreadstudio.com
email: order@thethreadstudio.com

Essential Textile Art
PO Box 167
Arana Hills
Queensland 4054
www.essentialtextileart.com
email: susan@essentialtextileart.com

Silk tops
Jacinta Leishman
Spiral Dyed Fibre & Thread
PO Box 277
Warrandyte, Victoria 3113 Australia
Phone: 03 9844 4104
International: +61 3 9844 4104
www.spiraldyed.com
email: Jacinta@spiraldyed.com

Threads and stabilisers
Embroidery Source
205 Fulham Road
Fairfield, Victoria 3078 Australia
Phone: 03 9499 9492 Freecall: 1800 137 670
International: +61 3 9499 9492
www.embroiderysource.com.au
email: enquiries@embroiderysource.com.au

About the Author

Eileen worked as a primary school teacher for a total of 22 years. She has an interest and expertise in many crafts including weaving and related textile arts, fabric printing, bookbinding, calligraphy and photography. She began patchwork and quilting in 1984 and since 1993 has been working as a textile artist, giving workshops and lectures both in Australia and overseas.

Eileen has written two books, *Appliqué Applied* and *Creative Medieval Designs for Appliqué* (originally titled *U is for Unicorn*), made videos and designs patterns for sale.

Her quilts have won many awards in Australia and overseas. She had quilts included in two Husqvarna Viking International Challenges, 'Feel Free', and 'Color, Couleur, Colore, Kulor'.

Her quilt *Pelican Twilight* won 'Best of World' in the 2002 World Quilt and Textile Competition (USA).

Iris Variations won 'Best Machine Workmanship' Innovative section in the 2007 World Quilt and Textile Contest (USA).

She was an invited artist for the 2004 Japanese travelling exhibition 'Contemporary Images in Japanese Quilts', and a contributor to the 2006 'Three Countries Challenge' (Japan, Australia and France).

Eileen specialises in machine work using appliqué, embroidery and quilting techniques. Her designs usually incorporate flora and fauna, whether from nature or imagination. Her work is often embellished with beads, braids and fabric paints, and machine quilted.

Eileen may be contacted by email at: eileen@herplace.net